UNITY IN DIVERSITY

THE INCREDIBLE INDIA

SULEKHA GUJJAR

Contents

Hinduism - Origin. 7

Hinduism - Significance. 9

Fundamental Tenets of Hinduism.. 13

Four Purusharthas. 14

Karma and Rebirth. 15

Samsara and Moksha. 16

God and Soul 17

Stages of Life and Rituals in Hinduism.. 19

Caste System in Hinduism.. 21

Sacred Scriptures of Hinduism.. 23

Four Sects of Hinduism.. 25

Vaishnavism.. 25

Shaivism.. 26

Shaktism.. 26

Smartism 26

Spread of Hinduism.. 27

Important Movement under Hinduism.. 30

Brahmo Samaj. 30

Arya Samaj. 32

Vardhaman Mahavira (539- 467 B.C.). 35

Teachings of Mahavira. 37

Spread of Jainism: 40

Division of Jainism: 41

Jain Councils/ Sangeeti: 42

The Legend of Shakyamuni 43

The Basic Tenents Of Buddhism.. 48

A. The *Dharma*, Reincarnation, and *Karma*. 48

B. The Four Noble Truths. 49

C. Nirvana. 50

D. How to Achieve *Nirvana*. 51

E. Bodhisattvas. 53

India During Buddha's Lifetime. 54

Buddhist Texts. 56

A. History. 57

B. Pure Land and Chan Buddhism.. 60

C. Tibetan Buddhism.. 62

The Spread of Buddhism.. 64

Introduction. 74

Philosophy and Beliefs. 76

History and Practices. 78

The Ten Gurus in Sikhism.. 83

Guru Nanak Dev – Guru from 1469 to 1539:. 84

Guru Angad Dev – Guru from 1539 to 1552:. 85

Guru Amardas Sahib – Guru from 1552 to 1574:. 86

Guru Ram Das – Guru from 1574 to 1581:. 87

Guru Arjan Dev – Guru from 1581 to 1606:. 87

Guru Har Gobind Sahib – Guru from 1606 to 1644:. 88

Guru Har Rai Sahib – Guru from 1644 to 1661:. 89

Guru Har Krishan Sahib – Guru from 1661 to 1664:. 90

Guru Tegh Bahadur Sahib – Guru from 1665 to 1675:. 90

Guru Gobind Singh Sahib – Guru from 1675 to 1708:. 91

Important Gurudwaras in Sikhism.. 91

The Sikh Literature:The Adi Granth and the Dasam Granth. 94

Christianity - Origin. 96

Christianity - Significance. 98

Tenets of Christianity. 100

Sects in Christianity. 103

Christianity in I

Unity in Diversity

The Incredible India

1.

Religion in India

Religion has historically influenced Indian society on a political, cultural and economic level. There is a sense of pride associated with the country's rich religious history as the traditions of Hinduism,

Buddhism, Sikhism and Jainism all emerged out of India. Moreover, while a majority of people in India identify as Hindu (79.8%), the medley of religions that exist within the country continually impact contemporary society.

In India, religion is more publicly visible than it is in most English-speaking Western countries. This becomes evident when considering the numerous spaces that are thought to be sacred and holy. Examples include 'ashrams' (monasteries or congregation sites) consisting of large communities of scholars or monastics, temples (mandir), shrines and specific landscapes such as the Ganges river. There is a rich religious history visible in architecture, and it is not uncommon to find various places of worship, such as a Hindu temple, Muslim mosque and Christian church, all next to each other.

The 2011 Indian census indicated that 79.8% of Indians identified as Hindu, 14.2% identified as Muslim and 2.3% identified as Christian. A further 1.7% of the population identified as Sikh, 0.7% identified as Buddhist and 0.37% identified as Jain.

Due to the massive population size of India, religious minorities still represent a significant number of people. For example, although only 0.37% of India may identify with Jainism, that still equates to over 4 million people. While not all religions in India can be discussed in detail, the following provides an overview of the major religions in the country as well as sizable religions that originated in India.

Hinduism in India

Hinduism - Origin

Hinduism does **not have a creator** or a **beginning date**. Most Hindu sacred scriptures have no **established authors** or dates.

Scholars define modern Hinduism as the result of approximately four thousand years of religious evolution in India, making it the world's longest surviving religion.

If, as some academics believe, the **Indus valley civilization** (3rd–2nd **millennium BCE**) was the earliest source of these traditions, Hinduism would be the world's oldest living religion.

Its many sacred scriptures in **Sanskrit and vernacular languages** served as vehicles for spreading the faith to various parts of the world, though ritual and the visual and performing arts also played a role.

Hinduism has had a stronghold in **Southeast Asia from the 4th century CE**, and it has lasted for almost 1,000 years.

The early holy scriptures of Hinduism, dating from around **1200 BC**, were largely concerned with the ritual sacrifices linked with a variety of gods who represented natural forces.

With the **Upanishads** and the formation of the **Vedanta philosophy**, a more philosophical orientation began to emerge around **700 BC**.

The majority of Hindus believe in a **Supreme God** whose traits and forms are reflected by the many deities who radiate from him.

Hinduism - Significance

Beginning with the Greeks and Persians, early visitors to the Indus valley referred to the locals as "Hindus" and in the 16th century, Indians themselves began to use the word to distinguish themselves from the Turks.

Gradually, rather than ethnic, geographic, or cultural differences, the divergence became largely religious.

Most otherworldly religions have definite dogmas, but Hinduism does not, and the common name "Hindu" encompasses a wide range of views.

Sacred writings do, however, give a set of beliefs and life orientations that are universally shared.

New writings were added to the Hindu tradition over time, marking the evolution of Hinduism as a living, evolving system of beliefs and activities.

Hinduism is a religion founded on Vedic concepts. The Vedas are also the Hindu religion's holy writings. The Vedas are divided into four sections.

The Rig-Veda, Yajurveda, Samaveda, and Atharvaveda are four Vedic texts.

Each Veda has subcategories, and it is in these four Vedas that the entire Hindu philosophy is written.

Hinduism, unlike **Christianity and Islam,** does not have a single text, such as the **Bible or the Quran.** Hinduism is likewise difficult to describe due to the lack of a single book.

The **Rig-Veda** is an ancient Indian text. It is a compilation of 1028 verses of Sanskrit poetry produced by Brahmin priests of the nomadic pastoralist Aryan peoples that entered India between 1500 and 1200 BCE.

It is the oldest and most venerated of the four Vedic texts.

Many early gods are mentioned in these passages, including

Agni, the deity of many types of fire;

Indra, the male god of rain and fertility;

Surya, the sun god; and

Varuna, the world's sovereign who ensures that the cosmic law is upheld.

Music, dance, and acting are all mentioned as ways of worship. Animal sacrifices on sacred altars are also a part of Vedic ritual.

The Rigveda speculates on the origins of the world and the meaning of life in it, although it does not claim to provide definitive answers.

Fundamental Tenets of Hinduism

The primary goal of human life is to get closer to God so that one's soul can be freed from the cycle of **human misery, death, and rebirth and achieve divine union.**

Despite no **conquest or conversion,Hinduism** has undergone reforms and has weathered immense adversity to become the third-largest religion.

Hinduism recognises and encourages numerous paths to **spiritual experience,** and is known for its tolerance of other religions, viewing them as merely different paths to the same end.

Because of this tolerance for diversity, it's difficult to pinpoint religious ideas that are **uniquely Hindu,** yet there are a few key elements that distinguish Hindu thought and practice.

Four Purusharthas

The Purusharthas are the four ends or goals of human existence. Individuals may have unique talents in one of the Purusharthas, but it is regarded that human life necessitates the pursuit of all four objectives.

Dharma - the ethical, duty-driven manner of living in cooperation with one's fellow human beings. This path includes a comprehensive set of rules for the "**right way of living.**"

Artha - the pursuit of material goods through productive labour For Hindus, Artha comprises not only traditional daily sustenance labour, but also government and civic service.

Kama - the exertion of desire and passion in the pursuit of pleasure and happiness. This does not imply hedonistic pleasure, as it does in some other faiths, but is seen as one aspect of a well-rounded spiritual life.

Moksha - the search of spiritual enlightenment and salvation This is the subject of scientific research and meditation, as well as various forms of mysticism.

Karma and Rebirth

Hindu tradition, like Buddhism, which arose from Hindu philosophy, holds that one's current state and future conclusion are the product of action and consequence.

Whether karma and rebirth from one lifetime to the next are considered as actual, deterministic events or psychological representations of living by consequences, Hinduism is a religion based on the merits of free-will activity rather than divine grace.

What you have done determines who you are in Hinduism, and what you do now determines who you will become.

Samsara and Moksha

Hindus believe that the condition of samsara is endless rebirth, and that the ultimate aim of life is moksha or nirvana - the realisation of one's relationship with God, the attainment of mental peace, and detachment from earthly worries.

This realisation liberates one from samsara, bringing a stop to the cycle of reincarnation and misery.

Some Hindu schools believe that moksha is a psychological condition that can be attained on Earth, but others believe that moksha is an afterlife release that occurs after death.

God and Soul

Hinduism includes a complicated belief system in both the human soul and a universal soul, which might be conceived of as a single deity—God.

Hindus believe that all living things have a soul, or true self, known as atman.

There is also a supreme, universal soul known as Brahman that is distinct and distinct from the individual soul.

Depending on the sect, different schools of Hinduism may worship the Supreme Being as Vishnu, Brahma, Shiva, or Shakti.

Life's objective is to comprehend that one's soul is identical to the supreme soul, that the supreme soul is present everywhere, and that all life is related in oneness.

In Hinduism, there are many gods and goddesses who represent the one abstract Supreme Being, or Brahman.

The Trinityof Brahma, Vishnu, and Shiva are the most fundamental Hindu deities.

However, many more gods and goddesses, including Ganesha, Krishna, Rama, and Hanuman, and goddesses such as Lakshmi, Durga, Kali, and Saraswati, are popular among Hindus all over the world.

Stages of Life and Rituals in Hinduism

According to Hindu mythology, human life is divided into four stages, each with its own set of rites and rituals from birth to death.

The First Ashrama, also known as the "Brahmacharya" or Student Stage

The Householder Stage, or the Second Ashrama—Grihastha

The Hermit Stage, or "Vanaprastha," is the third Ashrama.

The fourth Ashrama is known as "Sannyasa," or the Wandering Ascetic Stage.

In Hinduism, there are numerous rituals that can be performed at various stages of life and under a variety of circumstances, both in routine at home and during official festivities.

Devout Hindus observe daily rituals such as worshipping after bathing at daybreak.

On significant occasions, such as a Hindu wedding, Vedic ceremonies and hymn chanting are observed.

Other key life-stage events, such as ceremonies following death, include yaja and **Vedic mantra chanting.**

Caste System in Hinduism

The **Rig-Veda** also explains the mythic origins and rationale behind the caste system, which is one of the most distinguishing elements of Hindu life.

According to the **Rig-Veda,** caste originated with the sacrifice of a legendary creature called Purusha. He was divided into four pieces, each representing one of the major divisions of the caste system.

According to Hinduism, these divisions came into being through Lord Brahma, the creator of the cosmos.

In India, people are classified into four groups based on their caste: **Brahmins, Kshatriyas, Vaishyas,** and **Shudras.**

Caste status was hereditary, meaning it was passed down from father to kid at birth.

Each caste was subject to various local legal laws, with upper castes receiving more substantial rewards and being punished less severely than lower castes.

Sacred Scriptures of Hinduism

Vedas - The holiest of Hindu scriptures, which means "**divine knowledge.**" The **Rig-veda** (hymns and praises), **Yajurveda** (prayers and sacrificial rituals), **Samaveda** (tunes and chants), and **Atharva-Veda** (tunes and chants) are collections of writings created by the Aryans.

Upanishads - Philosophical treatises centred on the Brahma doctrine. Life is divided into four stages, as follows:

After rising from brahmachari (celibate students), grihasta (a householder) is the next step.

He becomes a vanaprastha (hermit) after a certain age, and the final stage of his existence is that of a sanyasi (an ascetic).

Brahmanas - Ritual and sacrifice instructions.

Bhagavad gita(God's Song) - It spans 18 books and 90,000 stanzas. The major civil war tale, as well as numerous sidebars, emphasise the effort to carry out one's responsibilities faithfully.

Four Sects of Hinduism

Vaishnavism

Vishnu is revered as the Supreme Lord by his devotees. **Bhagavatism,** commonly known as **Krishnaism,** may be traced back to the first millennium BCE.

There are numerous sampradayas, or sub-schools, under the Vaishnava tradition.

Shaivism

Shiva is revered as the Supreme Lord.

Shaivism can be traced back to the Vedic deity Rudra in the second millennium BCE, preceding **Vaishnavism.**

Shaktism

It elevates the feminine and the Devi, or goddess, to a position of supremacy. It is well-known for its **Tantra sub-traditions.**

Smartism

It is based on the Puranas' teachings.

They believe in the worship of five deities, **Shiva, Shakti, Ganesh, Vishnu, and Surya,** who are all worshipped equally in their homes.

Smartism recognises two types of Brahman: **Saguna Brahman** (a Brahman with qualities) and **Nirguna Brahman** (a Brahman without attributes).

Spread of Hinduism

During the **medieval period**, Hinduism experienced a **Bhakti movement in North India**, in which saints translated Sanskrit texts into vernacular languages and spread the message of Bhakti, or devotion to the Gods, to the masses.

The **Vaishnavite movement** was very strong in **South India** and reigned until the **end of the 13th century**. These saints, known as **Alvars**, were Vishnu devotees who sang songs that were collected and turned into **prabhandas**.

The **Shaivites**, or those who worshipped Shiva, were another powerful group in the South. The saints who followed were known as '**Nayanars**,' and we know of 63 major saints among them.

Outside of India, Hinduism did not normally attract or seek converts, although Southeast Asia was an exception.

As in southern India, the conversion movement began as a political movement.

From the **third century CE** through the **fourteenth century CE**, the powers of the Hindu temple and the Brahmin priesthood were transplanted to Southeast Asia to confirm royal authority.

Indian sailors brought cargoes to and from Burma (Myanmar), the Straits of Malacca, the **Kingdom of Funan** in modern Cambodia and Vietnam, and

Java in modern Indonesia as far back as **150 B.C.E** helped the spreading of Hinduism.

Sanskrit was spoken, and irrigation and farming technologies from India were used.

Sanskrit had expanded by the **fifth century**. Indian calendars were used to keep track of dates, and Indian gods such as Shiva and Vishnu, as well as depictions of the **Buddha, were worshipped.**

Important Movement under Hinduism

Brahmo Samaj

It started with **Raja Ram Mohan Roy**, who wanted to question Hinduism's problems.

In order to address these issues and discover the truth of Vedanta, he founded the **Brahmo Samaj in 1828.**

It was **opposed to iconography** and the worship of any kind of imagery.

It spoke out against Sati's evil practises, which were later abolished after years of campaigning.

Two schools were established by him to bring education to the masses

Movement by Swami Vivekanand and Ramakrishna Mission

Some movements, such as the **Ramakrishna Mission**, focused on changing Hindu philosophies from within.

It advocated unwavering devotion to God. It was stated that God could be formless or in the form of an object, but man's purpose is to find him. This is sometimes referred to as **'neo-Hinduism.'**

Swami Vivekananda, also known as **Narendra Nath Dutta**, was one of his most ardent supporters.

They desired that man combine his physical strength with his mental strength in order to bring about change in Hinduism.

The Ramakrishna Mission was founded in **1897** with **three goals in mind:**

to spread Vedantic spirituality;

to strive for the harmonious coexistence of all world religions, and

to consider service to mankind to be service to God.

Arya Samaj

Swami Dayanand

Saraswati founded it with the goal of reviving Hinduism from within.

They believed in the Vedas' supremacy and claimed that they were the repository of all values and knowledge.

One of their main policies was to work for the good of humanity.

They believed in the importance of education for the masses and established a large number of schools.

They practised iconoclasm and sought to convert non-Hindus to Hinduism.

He initiated the Suddhi, or purification, movement, which enabled the conversion to take place.

JAINISM IN INDIA

In the sixth century BC, India witnessed the rise of two new religions – Jainism and Buddhism. The primary reason for the rise of these religions was the religious unrest at that time in the country. This unrest was attributed to the rituals and sacrifices advocated by the Later Vedic period which were not understood by a larger section of people. The Rise of Jainism in India was a result of a mixture these factors.

The Jain Tradition

The Jain tradition had a succession of tirthankars(religious leader).

The first Tirthankar was Rishabha Dev.

The 23rd Tirthankar was Parshavanath who founded Jainism.

According to the Jain tradition, time is infinite and constituted by upward and downward movements. The tirthankars appear in succession in time, to teach the about the way of release of soul from material entanglements of this world.

Vardhaman Mahavira (539- 467 B.C.)

Vardhamana Mahavira was the 24th **Tirthankar** of the Jain tradition. He is considered the last tirthankar.

He was born at Kundagrama near Vaisali in about 546 BC.

He was born to Kshatriya parents Siddhartha and Trisala.

He was married to Yasoda and had a daughter from his marriage named Anojja or Priyadarsana.

He renounced the world at the age of thirty to become an ascetic and wandered for twelve years. He also practiced self-mortification for these years.

In the 13th year of his penance, he attained the highest spiritual knowledge by triumphing over himself. This knowledge is called **Kevala**

Gnan.

Thereafter, he was called Mahavira, Jina, Kevalin.

His followers were called the Jains and this religion came to be known as Jainism.

From this time till his death, he preached his doctrines for 30 years.

He **died** at the age of 72 at **Pava** near Rajagriha(now in Patna district).

Teachings of Mahavira

Jainism rejects the authority of Vedas and Vedic rituals.

It discards the belief in God.

Therefore, Jains don't worship God, but instead worship their tirthankars(their souls have attained salvation).

The 3 principles of Jainism are also known as **TriRatnas** (three gems) are:- – right faith, right knowledge, right conduct.

Right faith – It is the belief in the teachings and wisdom of Mahavira. Followers of Jainism are expected to have right faith.

Right Knowledge – It is the acceptance of theory which says there is no God and that the world has been existing without a creator, all objects possess a soul.

Right conduct – It refers to the observance of the five great vows:- not to injure life, not to lie, not to steal, not to acquire property, not to lead immoral life.

Everyone had to strictly follow the doctrine of Ahimsa.

Mahavira considered all objects, both animate and inanimate, to have souls and different degrees of consciousness.

He considered all objects to possess life and feel pain when they are injured.

Mahavira advocated a very holy and ethical code of life.

He considered even the practice of agriculture as sinful because it causes injury to the earth, worms and animals.

The doctrine of asceticism and renunciation was considered the shortest path to salvation by going to extreme lengths for the practice of starvation, nudity and other forms of self-torture.

Spread of Jainism:

Mahavira had organised the Sangha to spread his teachings, much like Buddhism.

He admitted both genders men and women in the Sangha.

Sangha consisted of both monks and lay followers.

The rapid rise of Jainism has been attributed to the dedicated work of the Sangha members who caused the spread of Jainism in Western India and Karnataka.

Jainism was patroised by rulers like Chandragupta Maurya, Kharavela of Kalinga and the royal dynasties of south India like the Gangas, the Kadambas, the Chalukyas and the Rashtrakutas.

Division of Jainism:

The division in Jainism happened by the end of the fourth century B.C.

A serious famine occurred in the Ganges valley. Various Jain monks led by Bhadrabagu and Chandragupta Maurya went to Sravana Belgola in Karnataka. These came to be known as Digambars(Sky-clad or Naked). They follow the tenets of religion strictly.

The monks who stayed back in north India were led by Sthulbahu, he changed the code of conduct for the monks. This sect became more liberal and started wearing white clothes. Hence, they came to be known as Swetambars(white-clad).

Jain Councils/ Sangeeti:

In 3rd century B.C , the first Jain Council was convened at Pataliputra headed by Sthulbhadra.

In 5th century A.D , the second Jain Council was held at Vallabhi in Gujarat under the Devardhigani. Here the compilation of Jain literature called Twelve Angas was completed

Buddhism In India

Buddhism, one of the major world religions, began in India around the sixth century, B.C.E. The teachings of Buddhism spread throughout Central and Southeast Asia, through China, Korea, and Japan. Today, there are Buddhists all over the world.

The Legend of Shakyamuni

According to Buddhist tradition, Shakyamuni (a name meaning "Sage of the Shakya Clan") is the founder of Buddhism (he is also sometimes referred to as "Siddhartha Gautama"). Shakyamuni was born around 490 B.C.E. to a royal family who lived in a palace in the foothills of the Himalayas. From the moment he was born, Shakyamuni did not lead a typical life. For example, legend states that Shakyamuni was born from his mother's hip while she remained standing in a grove of trees. In his youth, Shakyamuni's father provided him with everything he wanted and encouraged him to excel in his studies. However, he would not permit Shakyamuni to leave the palace grounds. Shakyamuni grew up with many luxuries and married a beautiful princess, but he still was not happy. He longed to see what was beyond the palace gates, thinking that a clue to his search for the meaning of life lay beyond the safety and luxury of the palace.

At the age of 29, Shakyamuni left the palace on four separate occasions to explore. He was deeply affected by what he saw.

During his first trip outside the palace, he saw a very old man who was bent over and had trouble walking. As Shakyamuni passed by in his carriage, the old man peered up at him, his eyes squinting from his severely wrinkled face.

In his second outing, Shakyamuni observed a sick man, wailing in pain. During his third excursion, Shakyamuni came upon the still and lifeless body of a dead man. Shakyamuni was shocked and saddened by the sights of old age, sickness, and death.

During his fourth outing, he saw a wandering monk, a seeker of religious truth. These four outings and what Shakyamuni saw (old age, sickness, death, and a seeker of religious truth) are called the "Four Sights."

Meeting the monk inspired Shakyamuni to leave the palace, his wife, and his newborn son.

He wanted to understand more about life, why human beings suffered, and how one could help relieve suffering in the world. Thus, he began his religious quest.

Shakyamuni began his search for enlightenment. According to Buddhist belief, enlightenment is the experience of true reality, an "awakening" through which one could comprehend the true nature of things. Shakyamuni thought he could reach enlightenment by practicing asceticism, a lifestyle of severe discipline.

Sometimes he would not eat or drink for long periods of time.

After six years of enduring many hardships, Shakyamuni realized that he had not come to a deeper understanding of life. He realized that neither luxury nor starvation would lead to enlightenment and instead decided to follow a moderate path or the Middle Way. He went to a village called Bodh Gaya where he became awakened to a true understanding of life.

The moment of his enlightenment took place while he was seated in meditation under a tree. In his enlightenment, he gained the power to see his former lives, the power to see death and rebirth of all types, and finally the realization that he had eliminated all desires and ignorance within himself.

He had become a Buddha, a title meaning "awakened one." The Buddha gave his first sermon, known as the "First Discourse," explaining his realization to the group of ascetics with whom he used to practice. These men became his first disciples.

He continued to spread his knowledge throughout towns in India for 45 years thereafter, gaining increasing numbers of followers until his death at the age of 80.

The Basic Tenents Of Buddhism

A. The *Dharma*, Reincarnation, and *Karma*

Buddhists believe that human beings have the potential to become free from suffering by practicing meditation and cultivating a lifestyle prescribed by the Buddha. The Buddha gave many lectures before his death. His teachings are referred to as the *Dharma*.

The wheel is a very important symbol in Buddhism because it depicts the cycle of life and death. Buddhists believe that after beings die, they are reborn or reincarnated into a new form. This new form could be a deity, human, animal, some lower creature like a hungry ghost (a being with a small head and huge stomach, and therefore always hungry), or an inhabitant of hell. It is believed that all positive thoughts and actions cause good *karma* and may direct one into being reborn in a higher form. The consequences of one's negative deeds, bad *karma*, may result in rebirth in a lower form. This endless cycle of rebirth, called reincarnation, reflects the impermanent nature of human existence.

B. The Four Noble Truths

As part of the *Dharma*, Buddha taught about the Four Noble Truths. These are:

1. Life is suffering.
2. Suffering is caused by craving.
3. Suffering can have an end.
4. There is a path which leads to the end of suffering.

The Four Noble Truths form the basis of Buddhist thought. It is believed that suffering, in part, is due to the impermanence of life. Even if one is happy at a given time, this happiness is not permanent. Since it is believed that life is suffering, the ultimate goal in Buddhism is to end the cycle of suffering, the cycle of repeated death and rebirth. The achievement of this goal is called *nirvana.*

C. *Nirvana*

The goal of Buddhism is to become enlightened and reach *nirvana*. *Nirvana* is believed to be attainable only with the elimination of all greed, hatred, and ignorance within a person. *Nirvana* signifies the end of the cycle of death and rebirth. According to the Four Noble Truths, "life is suffering" so ending the cycle of rebirth is something to be desired. Some Buddhists think of *nirvana* as a type of heaven where there is no suffering; other Buddhists view *nirvana* as a state of mind free from suffering. According to Buddhist belief, a final *nirvana* is attained at the time of an enlightened being's death, and is no longer part of the cycle of reincarnation and death.

D. How to Achieve *Nirvana*

Buddhists believe that the path toward *nirvana*, called the Middle Way or the Eightfold Path, outlines how people should live in order to reach *nirvana*.

The Eightfold Path consists of three categories: moral conduct, concentration, and wisdom.

Moral conduct consists of:

1. right speech (refraining from falsehood, malicious talk, and abusive language)
2. right action (refraining from stealing, killing, and unchastity)
3. right livelihood (earning a living through proper means, not killing living beings, making astrological forecasts, or practicing fortune-telling)

Concentration consists of:
4. right effort (energetic will to prevent or get rid of evil and promote goodness)
5. right mindfulness (to be diligently aware, mindful, and attentive)
6. right concentration (to rid oneself of unwholesome thoughts and achieve pure equanimity and awareness)

Wisdom consists of:
7. right thought (selflessness and detachment, universal thoughts of love and nonviolence)
8. right understanding (understanding of things as they are, a full understanding of the Four Noble Truths)

E. Bodhisattvas

Some schools of Buddhism including those of Chinese Buddhism believe that becoming a *bodhisattva* is a more important goal for individuals than achieving *nirvana*. A *bodhisattva* is a being who has attained enlightenment, but vows not to enter into final *nirvana* until all living things are released from suffering. *Bodhisattvas* choose to be reborn so that they can continue to work to relieve the suffering of others and try to make them aware of the Buddha's teachings.

In China, *bodhisattvas* are sometimes worshiped as much as the Buddha. For example, the female *bodhisattva* Guanyin became widely worshiped in Buddhist temples throughout China. In Buddhism, Guanyin is the Chinese *Bodhisattva* of Compassion.

India During Buddha's Lifetime

Buddha's ideas applied to people regardless of their rank in life, and stated that individuals are in charge of their own destiny. These ideas were in stark contrast to the ideas that were dominant during Buddha's lifetime.

Buddha was born during a time when Brahmanism was the main religion in India. Among other practices, Brahmanism encouraged the sacrifice of animals and the offering of gifts to Brahmanic priests for salvation.

The society at the time of Buddha's lifetime was also rigidly divided into castes. The caste system determined who people could marry, and what kinds of jobs they could have.

Buddhism differed in that it did not believe in social distinctions between human beings or claims to superiority based on birth. Buddhism was accessible to anyone. Buddhism also did not support animal sacrifices. In fact, Buddha believed that compassion should be cultivated among all living beings.

Buddhist Texts

After the death of Buddha, there was no one to take his place or to lead the new religion. Different schools of Buddhism formed, each with their own unique characteristics. Over the centuries, Buddhism has spread and changed. However, there are Buddhist works such as the *Pali Canon*, the "First Discourse" (Buddha's first speech after gaining enlightenment), as well as many *sutras* such as the Lotus *Sutra*, popular in China and Japan, that have provided important continuity to the religion.

Buddhism in China

A. History

When Laozi (the man credited as the founder of Daoism) left China to travel westward, some Chinese legends state that he traveled to India and became known as the Buddha. Although Buddhism was a religion that began outside of China, many countries, including China, adapted it and made it their own.

Merchants, traders, and Buddhist pilgrims helped spread Buddhist ideas to China by the second century C.E. Buddhism offered the Chinese new ideas such as *karma*, reincarnation, hell, monks, and monasteries. Buddhism encountered opposition in China, especially from Confucians, but was able to grow and thrive.

The Han Dynasty (202 B.C.E–220 C.E.), which had established Confucianism as their state doctrine, had collapsed by 220 C.E. The disorder caused by the collapse of the Han Dynasty made it easier for a religion such as Buddhism to be accepted because people, including the defeated Chinese aristocracy, became freer to choose their religious practices.

Buddhism and its ideas also provided comfort to many during this troubled and tumultuous time.

By the time of the Northern and Southern Dynasties (317–589 C.E.),

Buddhism had become established at all levels of Chinese society.

For a long period during the Tang Dynasty (618–907 C.E.), Buddhism was not only accepted in China, but it also flourished. Buddhist temples owned large amounts of land and did not have to pay taxes. Many Buddhist monasteries became very wealthy. When the Tang Dynasty fell on hard times, however, many Daoist and Confucian bureaucrats resented the wealth of the Buddhists. As a result, in 844–45 C.E., the government took Buddhist lands and profits away from them and destroyed their temples.

This persecution ended with the death of the emperor who had begun it.

Once again, Buddhism became accepted even though the temples did not regain their wealth. In the following years, Buddhism, Daoism, and Confucianism adopted aspects of each other's religious ideas and thoughts.

During the Cultural Revolution, Buddhism was once again suppressed. However, Buddhism and its influences still remain woven into Chinese culture.

B. Pure Land and Chan Buddhism

Buddhism in China was undoubtedly quite different from Buddhism as it was originally practiced in India. Two major schools of Buddhism that originated in China are Pure Land Buddhism and Chan Buddhism.

Pure Land Buddhism is based on the idea that buddhas or advanced *bodhisattvas* can create blissful paradises known as "Pure Lands." These pure lands can be reached through successful rebirths and devotion to the buddha of the pure land. According to tradition, there once was a king named Amitabha who became a monk after learning about Buddhism. When he became a buddha, he came into possession of the pure land called the Western Paradise. Individuals can supposedly reach the Western Paradise through devotion to the Amitabha Buddha. Calling the name of Amitabha, especially at the hour of one's death, is supposedly enough for an individual to ensure a rebirth in the Western Paradise.

Chan Buddhism developed in China in the sixth and seventh centuries. According to legend, the monk Bodhidharma was the first patriarch of Chan Buddhism. He is said to have meditated for nine years, cutting off his eyelids to stay awake. Chan Buddhism emphasized the importance of meditation in achieving enlightenment. Meditation, to the Chan Buddhists, was more important than *sutra* chanting, religious rituals, or worship of buddha images.

C. Tibetan Buddhism

Buddhism in Tibet is quite different from traditional Chinese Buddhism. Tibet adopted Buddhism centuries after China and did not model itself on Chinese Buddhism. Rather, in the seventh century, Tibet actively studied and imported aspects of Indian, rather than Chinese, civilization.[13] As a result, Tibetan Buddhism is closer to Indian Buddhism than Chinese Buddhism. Tibetan Buddhism also adopted many rituals of Bon, Tibet's native religion. Another unique characteristic of Tibetan Buddhism is how some lamas, including the Dalai Lama, are identified through reincarnation. Advanced lamas supposedly can know the identity of their rebirths. Many reincarnations of lamas have been found among the children of wealthy or influential patrons. These children are then trained and guided until they are ready to take on the responsibilities of a lama.[14] The Dalai Lamas are considered to be the manifestations of the *Bodhisattva* of Compassion, choosing to reincarnate and delay final nirvana to help humankind.

The Spread of Buddhism

Buddhism spread from India to China and also to other countries in Asia, such as Korea, Japan, Thailand, Myanmar (Burma), Sri Lanka, Cambodia, Laos, and Vietnam. Prince Shotoku of Japan, for example, wished to learn more about Buddhism to help Japan become stronger like the larger and more advanced China.

During the Tang Dynasty, Japan embraced Chinese Buddhism. This was just the beginning of Japan's adoption of many things Chinese, including China's system of government and bureaucracy.

Over the years, Buddhism has gained followers and has spread to other countries. China and other countries have adapted Buddhism to fit their own societies. Undoubtedly, this flexibility has contributed to its influence and longevity in the world.

Muslim in India

INTRODUCTION

Earliest Muslims came in India at Kerala/Malabar for trade. These Muslims were Arabs and their language was Arabic, settled down in Kerala and called as 'Moplas 'also called as 'Mappilas '. Let us first understand who were they and read a little more about them.

In west coast of Saudi Arabia, the holiest place was **"Mecca"** & in city of 'Mecca'in 570 AD.

Muhammad Prophet from (571 AD to 632 AD)

Prophet Mohammad was born when he was known during the time in Saudi Arabia, the people were divided into several tribes.

Prophet Muhammad belong to **"Quraysh"** tribe.

Gods in form of idols (Total 360 idols for different tribes). Example of Gods in South Arabia): Manaj, Uj, Lat .

When Muhammad Prophet was meditating in **'Hira Cave of South Arabia'**during course of meditation some revelation by angels were delivered to him.

This revelation by Allah is called as **"Revelation of the great "**.

Those who were idol worshippers were called as **believers.**

And non-idol worshippers were called as **non-believers.**

This was the beginning of the warfare between believers and non-believers.

Initially, believers were powerful and non-believers were less in number.

Rise of Islam

This is connected with migration of Prophet Muhammad from Mecca to Medina.

Gradually Islam became very popular in Saudi Arabia because of some social tactics. E.g. Economic Equality, Liberty & etc. This way Prophet Muhammad was able to gain some Banks of followers.

He went to Mecca and defeated all the Non-Believers in Mecca; all idols of Islam were destroyed. This was complete victory of Islam in Saudi Arabia.

After 622 AD, Islam was formally established in Saudi Arabia.

10 years later in 622 AD, Prophet Muhammad died.

Emergence of Sects

After his death within Islam there was a rise of two sects 'Shia & Sunni '. Majority of the Muslims of the world are Sunnis, India, Pakistan, Bangladesh etc.

Only in 4 Countries Shia are in majority these are Iran, Iran, Bahrain, Azerbaijan (Located in Central Asia).

The causes behind the emergence of the two sects were: Some wanted minority Muslims to be led by Ali ibn Abi Talib son in law of Muhammad Prophet (To spiritually lead them) and this sect came to known as Shia.

And others known wanted an elected person to lead them and gave him the title of **"Khalifa (Caliph) "**and these people emerged to be the second sect called as "Sunnis ". Abu Bakar Pbuh was the 1st Caliph.

Although all Muslims have groups consider the Quran to be divine, Sunni and Shia have different opinions on hadith.

These two groups often clash.

They have many disputes e.g. many personal laws like triple talaq is followed by Shia which aren't followed by Sunnis.

The reason behind these clashes is historical and ideological both.

Ali's entire family was killed by major Muslim group known as Sunnis

So in memory of this Shia celebrates **"Mohram "**, a festival remembering the people killed which is also celebrated in India .

Arab Invasion In India

Islam was established in Saudi Arabia and its followers came to known as Muslims.

Earliest Muslims came in India at **Kerala/Malabar** for trade.

These Muslims were Arabs and their language was Arabic, settled down in Kerala and called as '**Moplas** 'also called as 'Mappilas '.

These Moplas came in India when Muhammad Prophet was still alive (Came before 632 AD).

The first Mosque built by them was in 630 AD in Kodungallur(Oldest Mosque in India) ,these Muslims were purchasing spies (Black Pepper) in Kerala and were not rulers but traders .Later they became agriculturist (peasants) in Kerala

Mappilas peasants revolt occurred in 1921.

After Mopals the Muslim Invasion over India happened in 712 AD.

These Muslims were from Arab so, it is called as Arab invasion.

This happened in 2nd Decade of the 8th Century.

The first Muslim invader was Muhammad Bin Qasim (712 AD).

Qasim invaded Sindh (presently in Pakistan).

That time Dahir was the ruler of Sindh whose kingdom was invaded by him in 712 AD. An Arab vessel was Coming from Asia to Saudi Arabia with royal families of Arab. This ship was hijacked by pirates.

Al –Hejaz was the king of Arabia that time.

Dahir who was the king of Sindh did not respond to the request made by the king of Saudi Arabia to help and rescue the royal ship.

This resulted in sending a naval Expedition by attack over Sindh.

Dahir was easily defeated by Muhammad Qasim and he himself became the king of Sindh.

Muhammad Qasim started a new tax on not only non-Muslims (Majority were Hindus) which was a very controversial tax and it was imposed only in Sindh area.

Sikhism In India

Introduction

The word 'Sikh' in the Punjabi language means 'disciple'. Sikhs are the disciples of God who follow the writings and teachings of the Ten Sikh Gurus.

Sikhs believe in one God.

They believe they should remember God in everything they do. This is called simran.

There are over 25 million Sikhs worldwide, the great majority of them living in the Indian state of Punjab.

The Sikhs call their

faith **Gurmat** (Punjabi: "the Way of the Guru"). According to Sikh tradition, Sikhism was established by Guru Nanak (1469–1539) and subsequently led by a succession of nine other Gurus.

All 10 human Gurus, Sikhs believe, were inhabited by a **single spirit**. Upon the death of the 10th, Guru Gobind Singh (1666–1708), the spirit of the eternal Guru transferred itself to the sacred scripture of Sikhism, ***Guru Granth Sahib*** (The Granth as the Guru), also known as the ***Adi Granth*** (First Volume), which thereafter was regarded as the sole Guru.

Sikhism was well established by the time of **Guru Arjan**, the fifth Guru. Guru Arjan completed the establishment of **Amritsar as the capital of the Sikh world** and compiled the first authorised book of Sikh scripture, the Adi Granth.

Philosophy and Beliefs

There is **only One God**(*Ek Onkar "Ek" is One and "Onkar" is God)*. He is the same God for all people of all religions.

The soul goes through cycles of births and deaths before it reaches the human form. The goal of our life is to lead an exemplary existence so that one may merge with God.

Sikhs should remember God at all times and practice living a virtuous and truthful life while maintaining a balance between their spiritual obligations and temporal obligations.

The true path to achieving salvation and merging with God does not require renunciation of the world or celibacy, but living the life of a householder, earning an honest living and avoiding worldly temptations and sins.

Sikhism condemns blind rituals such as fasting, visiting places of pilgrimage, superstitions, worship of the dead, idol worship etc.

Sikhism preaches that people of different races, religions, or sex are all equal in the eyes of God. It teaches the full equality of men and women. Women can participate in any religious function or perform any Sikh ceremony or lead the congregation in prayer.

History and Practices

Guru Nanak preached a message of love and understanding and criticized the blind rituals of the Hindus and Muslims. Guru Nanak passed on his enlightened leadership of this new religion to nine successive Gurus.

Influences: The development of Sikhism was **influenced by the Bhakti movement and Vaishnava Hinduism.** However, Sikhism was not simply an extension of the Bhakti movement. Sikhism developed while the region was being ruled by the Mughal Empire. Two of the Sikh gurus – Guru Arjan and Guru Tegh Bahadur, after they refused to convert to Islam, were tortured and executed by the Mughal rulers. The Islamic era persecution of Sikhs triggered the founding of the Khalsa, as an order for freedom of conscience and religion.

The final living **Guru, Guru Gobind Singh established the Khalsa order** (meaning 'The Pure'), soldier-saints.

The Khalsa upholds the highest Sikh virtues of commitment, dedication and a social conscious.

The Khalsa are men and women who have undergone the **Sikh baptism ceremony** and who strictly follow the Sikh Code of Conduct and Conventions and wear the prescribed physical articles of the faith *(5K's: Kesh (uncut hair), Kangha (a wooden comb), Kara (a iron bracelet), Kachera (cotton underpants) and Kirpan (an iron dagger)).*

Sikhism does not have priests, which were abolished by Guru Gobind Singh. The Guru felt that they had become corrupt and full of ego.

Sikhs only have custodians of the Guru Granth Sahib (granthi), and any Sikh is free to read

the Guru Granth Sahib in the Gurdwara (a Sikh temple) or in their home. All people of all religions are welcome to the Gurdwara. A **free community kitchen** can be found at every Gurdwara which serves meals to all people of all faiths. Guru Nanak first started this institution which outlines the basic Sikh principles of service, humility and equality.

Four Rituals: "Sikh Rahit Marayada", the manual that specifies the duties of Sikhs, names four rituals that qualify as rites of passage.

The first is a **birth and naming ceremony**, held in a gurdwara.

A second rite is the **anand karaj** (blissful union), or **marriage ceremony**.

The third rite—regarded as the most important—is the **amrit sanskar**, the ceremony for initiation into the Khalsa.

The fourth rite is the **funeral ceremony**.

The three duties that a Sikh must carry out can be summed up in three words; Pray, Work, Give.

Nam japna: Keeping God in mind at all times.

Kirt Karna: Earning an honest living. Since God is truth, a Sikh seeks to live honestly. This doesn't just mean avoiding crime; Sikhs avoid gambling, begging, or working in the alcohol or tobacco industries.

Vand Chhakna: (Literally, sharing one's earnings with others) Giving to charity and caring for others.

The five vices: Sikhs try to avoid the five vices that make people self-centred, and build barriers against God in their lives. These are lust, covetousness and greed, attachment to things of this world, anger and pride

The Ten Gurus in Sikhism

The era of the ten gurus of Sikhism spans from the birth of Nanak Dev in 1469, through the life of Guru Gobind Singh.

At the time of Guru Gobind Singh's death in 1708, he passed the title of Guru to the Sikh scripture, Guru Granth.

Guru Nanak Dev – Guru from 1469 to 1539:

Guru Nanak Dev, first of the 10 gurus, founded the Sikh faith, introducing the concept of one God.

He started the institution of **Guru Ka Langar**. Langar is the term in the Sikh religion refers to the common kitchen where food is served to everyone without any discrimination.

He emphasized the equality of women and rejected the path of renunciation and he rejected the authority of the Vedas.

He was the **contemporary** of **Mughal emperor – Babur**.

Guru Angad Dev – Guru from 1539 to 1552:

Guru Angad Dev, second of the 10 gurus, invented and introduced the **Gurmukhi (written form of Punjabi) script**.

He compiled the writings of Nanak Dev in **Guru Granth Sahib in Gurmukhi Script**.

Popularized and expanded the institution of Guru ka Langar which was started by Guru Nanak Dev.

Guru Amardas Sahib – Guru from 1552 to 1574:

Guru Amardas introduced the **Anand Karaj marriage ceremony for the Sikhs**, replacing the Hindu form.

He established **Manji & Piri system** of religious missions for men and women respectively.

He strengthened the tradition of Guru Ka Langar.

He also completely abolished amongst the Sikhs, the custom of Sati and purdah system.

He was the contemporary of Mughal emperor – Akbar.

Guru Ram Das – Guru from 1574 to 1581:

Guru Ram Das, fourth of the 10 gurus, founded the city of Amritsar.

He started the construction of the famous Golden Temple at Amritsar, the holy city of the Sikhs.

He requested the Muslim Sufi, Mian Mir to lay the cornerstone of the Harmandir Sahib.

Guru Arjan Dev – Guru from 1581 to 1606:

He compiled the Adi Granth, the scriptures of the Sikhs.

He completed construction of Sri Darbar Sahib also known as Golden Temple in Amritsar.

He founded the town of Tarn Taran Sahib near Goindwal Sahib.

He became the first great martyr in Sikh history when Emperor Jahangir ordered his execution. Thus, he was hailed as Shaheedan-de-Sartaj (The crown of martyrs).

Guru Har Gobind Sahib – Guru from 1606 to 1644:

He was the son of Guru Arjan Dev and was known as a "soldier saint".

He organised a small army and became the first Guru to take up arms to defend the faith.

He waged wars against Mughal rulers Jahangir and Shah Jahan

Guru Har Rai Sahib – Guru from 1644 to 1661:

Though he was a man of peace, he never disbanded the armed sikh warriors who were earlier maintained by Guru Har Gobind.

He gave shelter to Dara Shikoh, the eldest son of Mughal Ruler Shah Jahan, who was later persecuted by Aurangazeb.

He cautiously avoided conflict with Emperor Aurangzeb and devoted his efforts to missionary work.

Guru Har Krishan Sahib – Guru from 1661 to 1664:

Guru Har Krishan was the youngest of the Gurus. He was installed as Guru at the age of five.

He was contemporary of Aurangazeb and summoned to Delhi by him under framed charges of anti-Islamic blasphemy

Guru Tegh Bahadur Sahib – Guru from 1665 to 1675:

He established the town of Anandpur.

He opposed the forced conversion of the Hindu Kashmiri Pandits by Mughal ruler Aurangazeb and he was consequently persecuted for this.

Guru Gobind Singh Sahib – Guru from 1675 to 1708:

He became Guru after the martyrdom of his father Guru Tegh Bahadur.

He created **the Khalsa in 1699**, changing the Sikhs into a saint-soldier order for protecting themselves.

Last Sikh Guru in human form and he passed the Guruship of the Sikhs to the Guru Granth Sahib.

Important Gurudwaras in Sikhism

Panj Takht: There are five Takhts and these Takhts are five gurudwaras which have a very special significance for the Sikh community.

Akal Takhat Sahib means Eternal Throne. It is also part of the Golden Temple complex in Amritsar. Its foundation was laid by Guru Hargobind Ji, the sixth Sikh Guru.

Takht Sri Keshgarh Sahib is situated at Anandpur Sahib, Punjab. It is the birthplace of the Khalsa, which was founded by Guru Gobind Singh in 1699.

Takht Sri Damdama Sahib is situated in the village of Talwandi Sabo near Bathinda. Guru Gobind Singh stayed here for about a year and compiled the final edition of Guru Granth Sahib, also known as the Damdama Sahib Bir in 1705.

Takht Sri Patna Sahib is situated in Patna city which is also the capital of Bihar state. Guru Gobind Singh Ji was born here in 1666 and he spent his early childhood here before moving to Anandpur Sahib.

Takht Sri Hazur Sahib in Nanded, Maharashtra.

Nankana Sahib (Pakistan): Birth place of Guru Nanak Dev.

Gurudwara Darbar Sahib (Kartarpur, Pakistan): Guru Nanak Dev spent the last 18 years of his life.

The Sikh Literature:The Adi Granth and the Dasam Granth

The *Adi Granth* is believed by Sikhs to be the abode of the eternal Guru, and for that reason it is known to all Sikhs as the *Guru Granth Sahib.*

The *Dasam Granth is controversial in the Panth because of questions concerning its authorship and composition.*

Value Of Sikhism

The Sikhs understand their religion as the product of five pivotal events.

The first was the teaching of Guru Nanak: His message of liberation through meditation on the divine name.

The second was the arming of the Sikhs by Guru Hargobind.

The third was Guru Gobind Singh's founding of the Khalsa, its distinctive code to be observed by all who were initiated.

At his death came the fourth event, the passing of the mystical Guru from its 10 human bearers to the *Guru Granth Sahib.*

The final event took place early in the 20th century, when Sikhism underwent a profound reformation at the hands of the Tat Khalsa.

Christian

Christianity - Origin

In the year 4 BC, Jesus Christ was born in Bethlehem as a Jew. He was thought to have superhuman abilities.

He began preaching to people in many towns and traveling far. Afraid of Jesus Christ's growing popularity and preaching, several Jewish priests plotted to assassinate him and succeeded in having him crucified.

Jesus was resurrected on the third day after His Crucifixion. He then ascended to heaven after another 40 days on earth.

The events leading up to and following his birth corresponded to Old Testament prophecies that the son of God would be born on the earth to atone for humanity's sins.

Following Jesus, his followers established a new faith known as Christianity (after Christ) and its adherents as Christians.

For the first time, the church was divided into two parts: Western, led by the people of Rome, and eastern, led by the **Patriarchates of Antioch, Alexandria, and Constantinople. Protestantism** shattered the Roman church.

According to the Saint Thomas Syrian Christians of Kerala, Thomas the Apostle is supposed to have brought Christianity to India in **52 AD** when he arrived on the **Malabar Coast of Kerala.**

Christianity - Significance

Christianity, one of the world's largest religions, has a sizable following in India.

It was formed in **Jerusalem by Jesus Christ**, and following his trial and three-day resurrection, it began to gain more and more disciples.

After some time, it became the Roman Empire's official religion and began to grow fast. **Vatican City** became the center of **Roman Catholic Christianity.**

After some time, numerous Christian reform movements emerged, and sects such as Protestants, Methodists, and others grew in popularity.

The Bible is the **Christians' holy book**. The **Bible** is a collection of **Hebrew, Aramaic, Greek, and English literature** dating from **9 BC to 1 AD.**

The Bible is divided into two parts: **the Old Testament**, which has 46 books, and the **New Testament**, which contains 27 books.

The Old Testament is a Hebrew scripture that offers information concerning the origin of the world and is important to both Jews and Christians.

The New Testament records Jesus Christ's life and teachings, which are at the heart of the **Christian faith.**

Tenets of Christianity

The **existence of one God** who created the Universe is central to **Christianity's philosophy.**

When it is essential, **God sends messengers or messiahs** to assist his creation. Jesus was a messenger sent to assist mankind in discovering God and becoming their **"savior."**

They also believe that God's presence was kept on Earth after Jesus died,

in the form of the **Holy Ghost or Holy Spirit.**

Christians worship the **Holy Trinity**, which includes the **Father (God), the Son (Jesus), and the Holy Ghost.**

The **Bible** is the Christians' sacred literature.

It includes Jewish elements of the Old Testament and a collection of new texts designated by the **Roman Catholic Church**, which is led by a

Pope.

The **New Testament** was the name given to this compilation, and it was combined with the **Old Testament to form the Bible.**

On Christmas, they commemorate Christ's birth and encourage people to gather in the hallowed place of prayer known as Church.

Baptism is one of their key practices, in which a child or anyone enters the church's service.

Another ritual is **Eucharist**, which entails breaking bread and wine with God to symbolize unity with the universe.

Christians believe that Jesus Christ **chose 12 learned men** to serve as his messengers and that he instructed them to spread his teachings and guide the people.

Peter (Simon), his brother Andrew, James, and his brother John, Philip and Bartholomew, sons of Zebedee, Thomas and Matthew, James, son of Alphaeus, Thaddaeus, Simon the Patriot, and Judas Iscariot, who betrayed Jesus Christ, are the 12 apostles.

Sects in Christianity

After Constantine, the Emperor of Rome, converted to **Christianity in 313 AD,** Christianity became the official religion of the **Roman Empire.**

With the **Roman Pope** as its leader, the religion was known as **Catholic or universal.**

Many divisions occurred by **1054 AD**, and the Church was formally divided into **Eastern Orthodox and Western Roman Catholic schools.**

A new school of thinking emerged in the **15th century**, challenging the Pope's power.

Martin Luther promoted various reforms in the Church in the **16th century**, resulting in yet another division in the Christian world and the establishment of Protestant churches throughout **Northeast Europe.**

Protestants opposed the Pope's authority and pushed for the Bible to be the exclusive source of authority.

Christianity in India

According to legend, **Christianity arrived in South India in 52 AD** with the advent of **St. Thomas**, one of Jesus Christ's apostles, on the Malabar Coast.

He lived in South India for a while and died near Madras. Others, however, claim that **Saint Bartholomew** was the first missionary to arrive in the country.

The **Portuguese** discovered a maritime passage between India and Europe in 1498, which resulted in commerce and cultural contacts between the two countries.

The Portuguese also impacted the **Mughal monarchs Akbar and Jahangir.**

In addition, the Portuguese attempted to convert **Mughal Emperors Akbar** and **Jahangir** to Christianity.

Christian scholars were also invited to the **Ibadatkhana,** which was erected by Akbar, for religious debate.

Christian preachers proceeded to visit Krishnadeva Rai, Vijay Nagar's most powerful monarch.

Christians began to arrive in India in this manner in medieval India.

The major turning point occurred in **1557**, when the Jesuit, **St. Francis Xavier**, elevated Goa to the rank of **Archbishopric**.

This phase of the missionaries, began in the **18th century** when they arrived in Bengal and influenced the religious climate by converting people.

The missionaries began to focus on providing **modern (English) education and medical assistance** to those who converted.

Even today, organizations such as the **Young Men's Christian Association (YMCA)** and the **Young Women's Christian Association (YWCA)** take the message of Christ to smaller tribal areas of India, where they convert locals and provide them with education and medicines.

several smaller denominations are active and flourishing, such as the Syrian Christians of Kerala, Protestant groups, and so on.

When the British government took over authority in India from the **East India Company in 1858**, the great period of Christian growth in India started. As missionaries, Christians from various countries arrived.

Christians are currently dispersed throughout India, with the majority residing in the Northeast, Kerala, and other southern regions.

In India now, there are 23 dioceses, 11 of which are located in Kerala.

Vlaues

Christianity is now the world's most popular religion. It has a global following of 2.168 billion people or around 31% of the world's population. With a population of 31.9 million people, it is India's third-largest religion after Hinduism and Islam. Following ongoing reforms that maintained the state system and economy independent from religion, Christianity has grown into a strong and established religion. As a result, it sets the way for human development on all levels

Evolution and other important aspects related to Christianity

Jesus Christ founded Christianity which spread throughout the Roman Empire where it was made state religion in 4th

The church split for the first time into- western under the people in Rome and eastern under the Patriarchates of Antioch, Alexandria and Constantinople. The Roman church was broken up by Protestantism.

According to the tradition of Saint Thomas Syrian Christiansof Kerala, Christianity was introduced to India by Thomas the Apostle, who is said to have reached the Malabar Coast of Kerala in 52 AD.

Some of the important beliefs associated with Christianity are:

Christians are **monotheistic**, i.e., they believe there's only one God, and he created the heavens and the earth.

This divine Godhead consists of three parts: the father (God himself), the son (Jesus Christ) and the Holy Spirit.

The **Holy Bible** includes important scriptures that outline Jesus's teachings, the lives and teachings of Major Prophets and disciples, and offer instructions for how Christians should live.

Both **Christians and Jews follow the Old Testament** of the Bible, but Christians also embrace the New Testament.

Some of the main themes that Jesus taught, which Christians later embraced, include: **Love God, Love your neighbor as yourself, Forgive others who have wronged you, Love your enemies, Ask God for forgiveness of your sins, Jesus is the Messiah and was given the authority to forgive others, Repentance of sins is essential, Don't be hypocritical, Don't judge others, The Kingdom of God is near. It's not the rich and powerful—but the weak and poor—who will inherit this kingdom.**

Contents

Printed by Libri Plureos GmbH in Hamburg,
Germany